NORTH AMERICAN ANIMALS

Long-tailed Weasels

by Rebecca Sabelko

BELLWETHER MEDIA • MINNEAPOLIS, MN

Note to Librarians, Teachers, and Parents:

Blastoff! Readers are carefully developed by literacy experts and combine standards-based content with developmentally appropriate text.

Level 1 provides the most support through repetition of high-frequency words, light text, predictable sentence patterns, and strong visual support.

Level 2 offers early readers a bit more challenge through varied simple sentences, increased text load, and less repetition of high-frequency words.

Level 3 advances early-fluent readers toward fluency through increased text and concept load, less reliance on visuals, longer sentences, and more literary language.

Level 4 builds reading stamina by providing more text per page, increased use of punctuation, greater variation in sentence patterns, and increasingly challenging vocabulary.

Level 5 encourages children to move from "learning to read" to "reading to learn" by providing even more text, varied writing styles, and less familiar topics.

Whichever book is right for your reader, Blastoff! Readers are the perfect books to build confidence and encourage a love of reading that will last a lifetime!

This edition first published in 2019 by Bellwether Media, Inc.

No part of this publication may be reproduced in whole or in part without written permission of the publisher. For information regarding permission, write to Bellwether Media, Inc., Attention: Permissions Department, 6012 Blue Circle Drive, Minnetonka, MN 55343.

Library of Congress Cataloging-in-Publication Data

Names: Sabelko, Rebecca, author.
Title: Long-tailed Weasels / by Rebecca Sabelko.
Description: Minneapolis, MN : Bellwether Media, Inc., 2019. | Series:
   Blastoff! Readers. North American Animals | Audience: Age 5-8. | Audience:
   Grade K to 3. | Includes bibliographical references and index.
Identifiers: LCCN 2017056262 (print) | LCCN 2018005319 (ebook) | ISBN
   9781626177987 (hardcover : alk. paper)| ISBN 9781681035239 (ebook)
Subjects: LCSH: Long-tailed weasel–North America–Juvenile literature.
Classification: LCC QL737.C25 (ebook) | LCC QL737.C25 S23 2019 (print) | DDC
   599.76/63–dc23
LC record available at https://lccn.loc.gov/2017056262

Editor: Betsy Rathburn   Designer: Josh Brink

Printed in the United States of America, North Mankato, MN.

Table of Contents

What Are Long-tailed Weasels?

Long-tailed weasels are **solitary** animals. They are found throughout southern Canada, the United States, and **Central America**.

N
W E
S

long-tailed weasel range =

conservation status: least concern

Extinct

Extinct in the Wild

Critically Endangered

Endangered

Vulnerable

Near Threatened

Least Concern

Long-tailed weasels live where they can find **prey**. They are found in fields, wooded areas, and backyards.

These **mammals** mark home
ranges using **scent glands**.
They may attack animals that
enter their range.

They make **burrows** in hollow logs, rock piles, and under buildings. Sometimes, they steal the homes of **rodents**.

burrow

Long-tailed weasels are named for their long, black-tipped tails. These can be over 11 inches (29 centimeters) long.

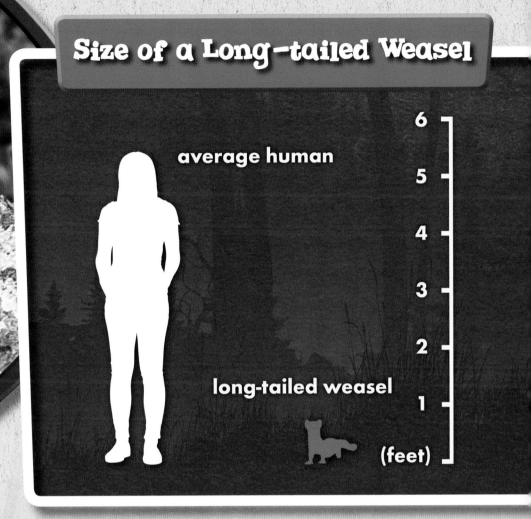

Size of a Long-tailed Weasel

average human

long-tailed weasel

6
5
4
3
2
1
(feet)

These weasels can reach up to 28 inches (71 centimeters) long. Their tails make up almost half their body length!

Long-tailed weasels have soft **undercoats** covered by brown outer hairs. They **shed** each spring and fall.

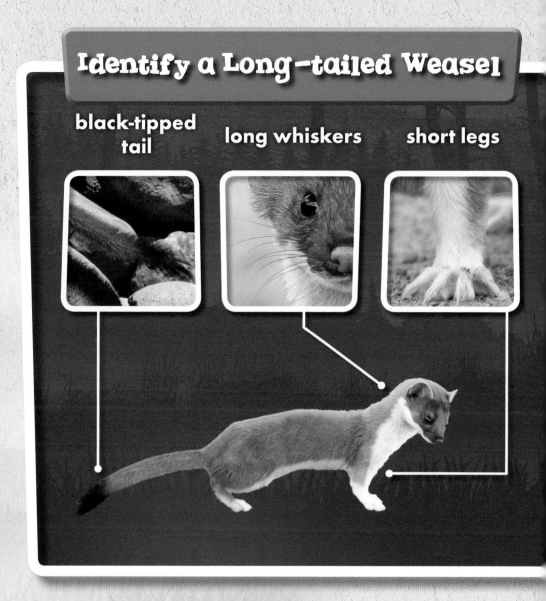

Identify a Long-tailed Weasel

black-tipped tail

long whiskers

short legs

In northern **climates**, their coats turn white during winter. The white fur helps them blend in with snow.

Fast and Fierce Hunters

Long-tailed weasels are quick and crafty **predators**. Long backs and short legs allow some to fit into animal **dens**.

When they enter dens, these weasels attack with strong claws and sharp teeth.

Long-tailed weasels are **carnivores**. They mostly feed on small mammals. Rabbits and mice are favorite foods.

On the Menu

American yellow warblers

eastern cottontails

white-footed mice

pocket gophers

ground squirrels

cliff chipmunks

Females are smaller than males. Their size helps them enter rodent homes. Large males often chase rabbits.

Long-tailed weasels are fierce critters. But these predators are hunted, too.

coyotes

Eastern Massasauga
rattlesnakes

great horned owls

red foxes

Coyotes and rattlesnakes often
chase them down. Sometimes,
owls carry them away!

Spring Pups

pup

Each spring, females give birth
in their cozy burrows. They have
about six helpless **pups**. The pups
are born with their eyes closed.
They have pink skin and white fur.

Baby Facts

Name for babies:	pups
Size of litter:	4 to 8 pups
Length of pregnancy:	280 days
Time spent with mom:	about 2 months

Long-tailed weasel pups grow quickly! They are able to hunt on their own after two months.

Soon, they are ready to say goodbye to mom. The pups scamper off to find their own homes!

Glossary

burrows—holes or tunnels that some animals dig for homes

carnivores—animals that only eat meat

Central America—the narrow, southern part of North America

climates—the specific weather conditions for certain areas

dens—sheltered places

mammals—warm-blooded animals that have backbones and feed their young milk

predators—animals that hunt other animals for food

prey—animals that are hunted by other animals for food

pups—baby long-tailed weasels

rodents—small animals that gnaw on their food

scent glands—body parts that produce smells; scent glands are located near long-tailed weasels' tails.

shed—to lose something on the body at the same time every year; long-tailed weasels shed their fur.

solitary—living alone

undercoats—layers of short, soft hair or fur that keep some animals warm

To Learn More

AT THE LIBRARY

Rathburn, Betsy. *River Otters*. Minneapolis, Minn.: Bellwether Media, 2018.

Sabelko, Rebecca. *American Badgers*. Minneapolis, Minn.: Bellwether Media, 2019.

Shaffer, Jody Jensen. *Black-footed Ferrets*. Mankato, Minn.: Child's World, 2015.

ON THE WEB

Learning more about long-tailed weasels is as easy as 1, 2, 3.

1. Go to www.factsurfer.com.

2. Enter "long-tailed weasels" into the search box.

3. Click the "Surf" button and you will see a list of related web sites.

With factsurfer.com, finding more information is just a click away.

Index